Chinese Chopsticks

by Lan Xiang

Foreign Languages Press

Writer: Lan Xiang

Translated by Chen Lin
Illustrations by Li Shiji
Designed by Yuan Qing, et al.
Managing editor: Lan Peijin

First Edition 2005

Chinese Chopsticks

ISBN 7-119-03852-4

© Foreign Languages Press

Published by Foreign Languages Press
24 Baiwanzhuang Road, Beijing 100037, China
Home Page: http://www.flp.com.cn
E-mail Addresses: info@flp.com.cn
                          sales@flp.com.cn

Distributed by China International Book Trading Corporation
35 Chegongzhuang Xilu, Beijing, 100044, China
P.O. Box 399, Beijing, China
Printed in the People's Republic of China

Contents

Preface

In the brilliant long history of Chinese culture, popular culture holds an important place. It is an invaluable companion of literary culture as well as being of independent social value. In the development of the Chinese nation, popular, or folk culture, and literary culture jointly create the image of, and foster the spirit of the nation. As for the modes of expression, folk culture shows a fresher, clearer and a more vivid and lively style. It is like a mirror reflecting the life and social customs of a nation or a region.

From either concrete instruments or abstract rites and customs, one may discern how the ancestors of today's Chinese people created this marvelous culture. One can almost feel their purity, hear their compassionate voice as well as witness their meticulous craftsmanship. Their adroit creations are enlightening today and their pursuit of melodious sounds and miraculous aesthetics is a pleasure for us later generations to follow and enjoy.

Popular culture exists everywhere. Many instruments and actions, displaying rich cultural value, developed into common rules and laws in due course. This book is about chopsticks culture, which is a component part of the Chinese popular culture. Chopsticks are dining tools of the Chinese people. The two thin and long sticks are mostly made of either bamboo or wood. One just uses the thumb, forefinger and middle finger dexterously to pick up food by opening and closing the two chopsticks. Such simple and common tools, however, embody rich culture.

Chinese people's use of chopsticks as a dining tool traces back to ancient times. Today they are called *kuaizi*, in those days they were called *zhu*. By dissecting the Chinese character of *zhu*, one finds the top radical means bamboo, which shows that they were first made of bamboo and the bottom means cooking in utensils. Hence it seems logical that chopsticks came into being at the same time as humans learned to eat cooked food. In early times people might have used two bamboo sticks or twigs to pick up food from utensils. It was basically to prevent the fingers from getting greasy and dirty and to prevent them from getting burned by the hot food. Over time chopsticks finally became the fine handicrafts we see today. Thanks to their simple design and easy application, chopsticks in no time became popular and spread far and wide. Nowadays, chopsticks are common dining tools, not only used by the great majority of the Chinese people, but also by some peoples and nations in Northeast and Southwest Asia and to an extent internationally. Besides the practicality and vitality, chopsticks meet with scientific theory. Some scholars extol the chopsticks that are used by the Chinese people as a proud and encouraging scientific innovation. The famous physicist Dr. Tsung Dao Lee, a Chinese American, once wrote about chopsticks, suggesting that such two simple things superbly apply the leverage theory of physics. They are an extension of human fingers, and they can do whatever fingers can, fearing neither heat nor cold. He claimed that chopsticks are simply fantastic. A Japanese scholar made the following scientific finding on chopsticks: "Using chopsticks to pick up food involves the movement of eighty-odd joints and fifty muscles in the shoulder, arm, palm and finger. Moreover, they also involve the cerebra-nerve. Thus, dining with chopsticks forces man to have an adroit hand as much as trains the brain to function cleverly and keeps a healthy body."

The characteristics of chopsticks may be summed up as simplicity, practicality, refinement and science.

The Origin and Development of Chopsticks

Chopsticks are an internationally recognized exclusive dining tool. Westerners, who are used to knives and forks, indeed find it hard to master chopsticks but once they can operate the two little sticks they will find them very convenient and flexible. Hence some Western scholars commend them as a representation of ancient Eastern civilization and the crystallization of the wisdom and intelligence of the Chinese people.

The Chinese people have a history of at least three thousand years of using chopsticks, and probably far longer because nobody knows the exact era when chopsticks came into being. Over one billion Chinese people everyday, three meals a day, use chopsticks, so they take it for granted as a matter of routine, without thinking about it. In history,

Chopsticks for eating Chiese food are usually made from wood, bamboo, animal bones or other materials. About 25 to 30 centimeters long, their top is square, about 0.8 square centimeter, and the low end round with a diameter of 3 to 5 millimeters.

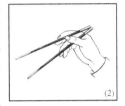

(1)

The correct way of using the chopsticks requires concerted efforts of the thumb, index finger, middle finger and third finger. Hold the pair of chopsticks in the right hand, using the index finger, middle and third fingers to keep the chopsticks steady near their top and then push them open by moving the thumb and index finger. (Drawing 1)

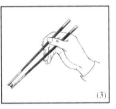

(2)

To pick things up with chopsticks, lift upward one of the two chopsticks with the index and middle fingers while keeping the other one where it is so as to separate the two. (Drawing 2)

Once the chopsticks have picked up the food, press one of the chopsticks with the thumb ad index finger and raise the pair. (Drawing 3)

(3)

there is very little written record about chopstick culture. If there is, there are only a few words or phrases in some ancient books, and they are not on chopsticks but only mentioned as a spin-off or by way of other things. For thousands of years no one has specialized in the study of chopsticks. Today, chopstick culture, just like all Chinese culture, attracts people from all over.

The earliest record of Chinese chopsticks appeared around the 11th century BC. According to *Han Feizi*, Emperor Zhou used ivory chopsticks for every meal. Emperor Zhou, the last ruler of the Shang Dynasty (17th- 11th century BC), reigned from 1075 to 1046 BC. This proves that chopsticks have a history of at

Emperor Zhou ordered elephant hunts.

least three thousand years. As an aside, there were herds of wild elephants in central China three thousand years ago. Archaeologists found written records about elephants and catching elephants and so it is quite plausible that Emperor Zhou used ivory chopsticks.

The fact that Emperor Zhou used ivory chopsticks for every meal became a major historical event, as recorded in *The Book of History* and *Han Feizi*. This was because three thousand years ago, weapons and production tools were very primitive, and the hunting of elephants and harvesting of ivory were a major event in those days. It consumed huge amounts of labor and finances as well as costing many lives.

We are sure that the chopsticks that Emperor Zhou used were by no means the first pair, they must have come into being years before him. As for when the first pair was made and who invented them, there is no written record. However, a folktale may offer some insight into the making of the earliest chopsticks.

According to the legend, in the Xia Dynasty (2070-1600 BC), the Great Yu was leading a team of people to prevent the river from flooding. He was so busy with the work that he did not go back to his home though he passed his house gate three times. They were all eating along the riverside and did not know how to fish out the food from the cooking pot, so Great Yu broke two twigs from a tree branch and picked up meat and vegetables from the boiling pottery pot. Along with the passage of time, the prototype of chopsticks took shape.

The footnote made by Zheng Xuan to the text of *The Book of Rites* says that ancient Chinese wrapped up corncobs with leaves and clay and then roasted them on a fire while turning them around with twigs. When they were cooked, people would use twigs to pick the corn out of the fire and also to take off the wrapping. This way of roasting food certainly would have helped the development of chopsticks. Contemporary scholars like Luo Zhufeng reason that the history of the Chinese people using chopsticks can date back to the Xia Dynasty (2070-1600 BC).

All in all, the coming into being of chopsticks is not isolated. Spoons have been found in the excavation of the ruins of the Yangshao Culture of the Neolithic Age. In the late Neolithic Age, man's intelligence developed and living conditions improved, so just a spoon would not be enough for cooking and chopsticks naturally took shape. Nevertheless, in the Xia Dynasty some four thousand years ago, chopsticks were only in prototype. Through evolution, they took the shape of a pair of eighteen-centimeter-long sticks in the early Shang Dynasty, which led later to Emperor Zhou ordering elephant hunts to procure ivory for chopsticks.

Chopsticks have had many a name. In the

Cylindrical chopsticks of the Western Han Dynasty excavated in Changsha, Hunan, in 1973.

early Qin Dynasty over two thousand years ago, they were called *Jia* and in the Han Dynasty (206 BC- AD 220) also called *zhu* but a different character (top radical meaning bamboo and bottom meaning assistance). Later in the Tang, Song, Yuan, Ming and Qing dynasties (618-1911), they were all named *zhu* (Bamboo on top and cook at bottom).

The Feast, a stone painting of the Han Dynasty, was excavated in Sichuan Province.

In this stone painting of the Han Dynasty unearthed in Shandong Province, a man in kneeling position feeds his father with chopsticks.

The name had some changes in the Ming Dynasty (1368-1644). Fishermen of Zhejiang Province took the word *zhu* as a particular taboo, because it shared the same pronunciation of the character of "stop" and "shipworm" and the fishermen feared that their business would stop and their boats would be eaten up by shipworm. Haunted by this superstition, they changed them into *kuaizi*, meaning quick, hoping for good fortune. Nowadays, they are universally called *kuaizi* and only some scholars use the character of *zhu* in their calligraphy and poems.

Dr. Tsung Dao Lee's description epitomized the physics theory of chopsticks. Chopsticks are indeed superb dining tools. For instance,

The stone painting of chopsticks and pickles dating to the Wei and Jin dynasties was excavated from tomb No. 7 in Jiayuguan, Gansu Province.

Chinese feel at ease and quite refined when eating noodles with chopsticks. The two sticks pass the noodles from plate to mouth easily while it is quite difficult to eat noodles with a fork. One has to turn the fork five or six times to gather the noodles to the mouth, with the head held low. It is even more inconvenient to eat noodle soup where they slip off the spoons or forks, spilling over the clothes and making the diner feel very awkward.

According to the study of gastronomy, in ancient times, the cook would peel and cut the food into chops or shreds and then serve the food at the table. This suited the use of chopsticks but others think it was done for quicker cooking and that chopsticks came into being afterwards.

Looking at pictures of real chopsticks may give a more vivid sense. Thanks to the unremitting efforts of archaeologists in the past fifty years, some chopsticks have been excavated from ancient tombs. Because chopsticks

Mural from No. 473 Cave of Dunhuang of the Tang Dynasty, depicting chopsticks and spoons laid out in front of five ladies

before the Qin Dynasty were mainly made of bamboo or wood, and decayed underground, there have been no findings of bamboo or wooden chopsticks from before the Qin Dynasty period.

The earliest non-bamboo chopsticks unearthed were a pair of bronze chopsticks excavated in Huijiachong of Anhui Province. Because of erosion through the years, the two chopsticks were a little bit different in length, averaging twenty centimeters. They were from the late Spring and Autumn Period (770-476 BC).The most famous bamboo chopsticks were the pair of seventeen centimeters unearthed in 1973 in Changsha, Hunan. This pair of over 2,100 years old round chopsticks dating to the Han Dynasty is on display in the Hunan Provincial Museum.

In fact, quite a lot of chopsticks of the Han Dynasty (206 BC-AD 220) have been found besides the pair in Hunan, including copper and bamboo chopsticks found in Hubei and Gansu provinces. The brick carved with Picture of a *Feast of the Han Dynasty*, which was excavated in Sichuan, carried images of chopsticks. Among the three diners sitting on the floor, the one on the left is holding a bowl with chopsticks standing in the middle of the bowl, and in front of the other two at the table there are two pairs of chopsticks. This showed that chopsticks were quite common in the Han Dynasty. Chopsticks of the Han Dynasty were round in shape and thick on top and thin at bottom. Chopsticks of the Spring and Autumn Period, however, were made of copper and were cylindrical. Because copper is easily oxidized silver chopsticks gradually replaced them.

A pair of silver chopsticks of the Sui Dynasty (581-618) excavated in Xi'an were twenty centimeters in length with thin heads at both ends and thick in the middle. They are the earliest silver chopsticks found in China so far.

In about three hundred years of the Tang Dynasty (618-907), Chinese feudal society developed to its heyday, politically, economically and culturally and the people's living standard improved enormously. Exchanges between China and other countries boomed and with the development of smelting technology gold and silver chopsticks often appeared at the dining table.

According to *Episodes of the Kaiyuan Period* of the Tang Dynasty, Song Jing was the Prime Minister. At the imperial spring banquet, the Emperor granted Song a pair of gold chopsticks as a reward. In those days, gold-wares were only allowed in the imperial court. Officials, no matter how high they were, to say nothing of the common folks, were forbidden to keep silver and gold privately. Gold-wares made privately were illegal. When Song Jing learned that the emperor bestowed him with gold chopsticks, he was so horrified that he did not know what to do. Seeing this, Emperor Xuanzhong said, "I am not giving you gold, but chopsticks to commend you as straight as the chopsticks." When Song heard this, he was deeply honored and moved to accept the gold chopsticks. This scrupulous prime minister never dared to use the gold chopsticks for meals but kept them in his residence. Silver chopsticks unearthed from the Tang Dynasty were mainly from the tombs of high officials, nobles and the upper class. The following table shows findings of silver chopsticks of the Tang Dynasty.

Silver chopsticks of the Tang Dynasty have

Excavation site	Quantity	Quality	Length (cm)	Features	Source
Luoyang, Henan Prov.	2	Silver	15		*Relics & Reference Data*, Issue No.5, 1956
Yanshi, Henan Prov.	2	Silver	15.8	Two holes on top, thick top & thin bottom	*Archaeology*, Issue No.10, 1984
Danyang, Jiangsu Prov.	36	Silver	22.2 to 32	Six of which carved with "Strongman"	*Cultural Relics*, Issue No.11, 1982
Yaoxian, Shaanxi Prov.	2	Silver	30		Cultural Relics, Issue No.1, 1966
Lantian, Shaanxi Prov.	3	Silver	33		*Archaeology and Relics*, Issue No.11, 1980
Changxing, Zhejiang Prov.	30	Silver	33.1		*Cultural Relics*, Issue No. 11, 1980

Picnic, a mural from a Tang Dynasty tomb unearthed in Xi'an

been unearthed in large quantities, with the longest at 33.1 centimeters. Those of the Spring and Autumn Period were only between 17 to 18 centimeters. Silver is a valuable metal and the length of the silver chopsticks reflects the prosperity of the Tang Dynasty.

The mural titled *Picture of a Banquet* in Cave No. 473 at Dunhuang shows that there were often elaborate banquets during the Tang Dynasty, at which there were chopsticks and spoons in front of everybody at the table in a pavilion. A mural from the tomb of the Tang Dynasty in Xi'an shows pairs of chopsticks besides glasses and plates.

Many chopsticks of the Song, Yuan, Liao and Xia dynasties were unearthed and they were made mostly of silver and copper. Compared with those of the Tang Dynasty they were shorter, around 25 centimeters and the shortest were only 15 centimeters. The finds so far have not produced any longer than 30 centimeters. The feature of the time was that their shape varied, while that of the Tang Dynasty and before was simple and cylindrical.

Two pairs of silver chopsticks of the Song Dynasty (960-1127), unearthed in Jiangxi Province, had transformed the traditional cylindrical shape into hexagonal, while silver chopsticks of the Song Dynasty, excavated in Sichuan, had different patterns on the chopsticks. From the Song Dynasty, chopsticks started to develop in craftsmanship. Silversmiths knew that they had to show their talents. The four silver chopsticks of the Yuan Dynasty (1271-1368) unearthed in Wuxi, Jiangsu Province, even had the names of the craftsman carved in them.

Over thousands of years, Chinese chopsticks culture has kept on developing. In the Ming Dynasty (1368-1644) there was a striking change of shape that turned into square on the top and round at the bottom and laid a foundation for fine craftsmanship. According to *Cultural Relics*, Issue No.7, 1980, one red painted wooden chopstick of the Ming Dynasty unearthed in the hanging coffin in Hongxian County of Sichuan Province was 28 centimeters long, with square top and round bottom. On the sides of the square top, there was a poem with a verse carved on each side.

One wooden chopstick of the Ming Dynasty found in a boat unearthed in Ningling of Henan Province was 31 centimeters long, with a square top and a round bottom. Excavation of the tomb of Emperor Shenzong of the Ming Dynasty in 1956 in Beijing yielded ebony chopsticks with gold plating on the top.

These imperial chopsticks also had square tops and cylindrical bottoms, with a gold cover on the top of the chopsticks.

Chopsticks of the Qing Dynasty were famous for their fine craftsmanship. Bamboo and wooden chopsticks with silver mosaic were common. The chopsticks of the Qing Dynasty conserved in the Shanghai Folk Arts Museum include ivory chopsticks with silver mosaic, Xiang courtesan bamboo chopsticks with silver mosaic, ebony bamboo with silver mosaic, hardwood chopsticks with silver mosaic. These silver mosaic chopsticks have silver veneer of 6 to 7 centimeters on the bottom part and the top part has silver cover with a 7- to 8-centimeter silver chain to keep the two chopsticks together. Chopsticks of the Qing Dynasty had silver mosaic on the top and bottom and some had a silver ring in the middle, which was depicted in Chapter 40 of the novel of *Dream of the Red Mansions*. But in the late Qing Dynasty, chopsticks with a silver ring in the middle were no longer fashionable and the top with a silver chain replaced it.

Varieties of Chopsticks

Ancient Chinese attached great importance to cuisine and the Chinese people have proved time and again that they offer delicious food. The making of chopsticks became more and more meticulous and artistic so as to satisfy emperors and their officials and nobles. Through the dynasties, however, very few people cared about the study of chopsticks culture. Through many years of study and research, I have collected 1,600 pairs of chopsticks, both modern and antique. After measuring and analyzing them with reference to records and history books, I have divided them into five categories, namely, bamboo and wooden chopsticks, metal chopsticks, ivory and bone chopsticks, jade chopsticks and plastic chopsticks.

(1) Bamboo and wooden chopsticks

When mentioning chopsticks people are most familiar with bamboo chopsticks and painted wooden chopsticks today. Ordinary families mostly use these kinds of chopsticks. Richer families may use hardwood chopsticks. Bamboo and wooden chopsticks are universal in China because the earliest chopsticks were made of bamboo

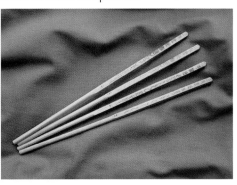

Mao bamboo chopsticks

Palm bamboo chopsticks
of the Yuan Dynasty

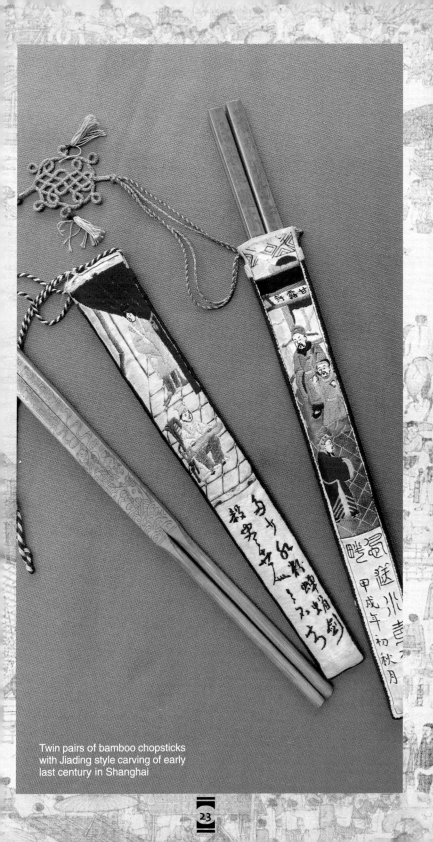

Twin pairs of bamboo chopsticks
with Jiading style carving of early
last century in Shanghai

and wood.

"Palm bamboo chopsticks" are precious. Palm bamboo chopsticks were rare among ancient chopsticks. Palm bamboo grown in the

Nan bamboo chopsticks

southeast of China had fine fibre and was hard. Chopsticks were first made out of it some six to seven hundred years ago because the material had grayish brown grains and was bright and smooth. When I first set my eyes on a pair of palm bamboo chopsticks with ivory cap from the Yuan Dynasty I liked them and bought them for my collection. They are 28 centimeters long and cylindrical with a 0.5 centimeter diameter. On the top, the bamboo and the ivory were mortised, and they still remain intact after hundreds of years, which showed the superb traditional craftsmanship of the time. On the upper part, they are carved

Palm bamboo chopsticks

with circular patterns, which was unique. Purple bamboo was also fine material for chopsticks, but antique purple bamboo chopsticks are rare.

"Xiang courtesan bamboo chopsticks". According to legend, when Emperor Shun was making inspections in the south, he suddenly passed away and was buried in the wild. Learning of the death, his two courtesans, Erhuang and Nuying rushed to the riverside of the Xiang River and cried their hearts out, their tears falling into bamboo bushes. The bamboo was imprinted with tear trace marks, so it was also named "tear-trace bamboo" or "Xiang courtesan bamboo". I have a collection of Xiang courtesan bamboo chopsticks of the Qing Dynasty. They are yellowish with a purple grain mark, natural, simple and graceful. They are 26 centimeters long, the bottom, 7.5 centimeter is silver plated and they have silver caps as well.

Courtesans Erhuang and Nuying, a picture story in the promenade of the Summer Palace in Beijing

"Bamboo chopsticks carved with lion head from Jiang'an of Sichuan". Bamboo chopsticks have one special feature.

Tear-trace bamboo chopsticks

That is they are easy to carve. Jiang'an of Sichuan Province, with a history of over three hundred years of chopsticks making, is famous for its carved bamboo chopsticks, and has won many international awards. The *Nan* bamboo of Jiang'an is thick and long between joints, which is ideal for making chopsticks. *Nan* bamboo is boiled in hot water, dried under the sun, polished and made

Carved bamboo chopsticks from Jiang'an

into chopsticks and finally images of lion heads are carved on the top of chopsticks. I have collections of lion-head chopsticks of this kind made in the early 20th century. A pair of vivid lion heads was carved on the top of the chopsticks. They are among the best of bamboo chopsticks.

Storksbill wooden chopsticks

"*Nan* bamboo chopsticks from Hunan" has

a different feature. If you put this kind of chopstick into the water and blow into it, bubbles will appear, because the bamboo has microscopic holes. These chopsticks will neither decay, nor get wormed or warped. When *Nan* Bamboo chopsticks are put into the water, they will stand straight and not lie flat and float on the water, thus they are nicknamed "magic chopsticks".

According to *Rites of the Zhou Dynasty*, on happy occasions, chopsticks and spoons made from hawthorn were used. This was because hawthorn shared the same pronunciation as "good omen". While chopsticks and spoons made from mulberry wood were used to serve guests at meals after funerals because the wood shared the same pronunciation as "deceased". Mulberry wood is yellowish white, which is the traditional color for observing mourning ceremonies. There is an illustrative story about a scholar named Fan Jin, who having passed the imperial examination, was invited by the county Magistrate Tang to a dinner to celebrate. The magistrate placed silver chopsticks for Fan, but he refused to be seated. Feeling that it was not solemn enough for the occasion, the magistrate replaced them with ivory chopsticks, and Fan still refused to be seated. When the magistrate learned that Fan Jin was observing the mourning ceremony for the death of his mother, he ordered white wooden chopsticks be placed in front of him. Only then did Fan seat himself at the dinner table. This shows that the etiquette on the use of chopsticks was exquisite, and no sloppiness was allowed.

"Hardwood chopsticks" are traditional top-class chopsticks. Hardwood chopsticks are simple, graceful and stately and match perfectly with top-class porcelain wares at dinners. Hardwood chopsticks in a box including five pairs of chopsticks with

Hardwood chopsticks

Ebony chopsticks

Cassia chopsticks

Coconut chopsticks

Boxwood chopsticks

Chinese ilex-wood chopsticks

patterns of pine-trees, turtle and crane, which stand for longevity, are carved on the box. It is an ideal gift for the aged.

"Ebony chopsticks" are the most valuable among wooden chopsticks. Ebony is native to Indonesia, Malaysia and Guangdong Province of China. The wood is hard, smooth, dark, heavy and durable. Ebony chopsticks with white porcelain tableware will make dinners very colorful.

"Red sandalwood chopsticks made by the Xian family" of Yuexiu District of Guangzhou, have a history of only eighty years, and the owner Xian Lianguang is the third generation of the craft. Today, these handmade hardwood and ebony chopsticks are still very popular in Guangdong and Hong Kong. Particularly the red sandalwood chopsticks with traditionally carved lion heads are exquisite wooden chopsticks, displaying the Xian family craftsmanship.

"Chinese ilex wood

chopsticks", compared with ebony chopsticks, are simple and graceful. Ilex wood is hard and fine with a cool fragrance. In northern Shaanxi Province, they are said to be good for the eyes, while folks in Henan Province say that they are good to prevent ulcers in the mouth. Another feature of ilex wood is that different patterns can be imprinted on the creamy white chopsticks with an electro-engraving pen.

Dark sandalwood chopsticks

Chicken-wing wooden chopsticks

"**Ironwood chopsticks**" are made from the iron tree (sago cycas) that grows in mountain rocks in Anhui Province. Ironwood is solid and heavy with fine grains. The peculiar feature of this kind of chopsticks is that they sink in water, indicating the solidness of the wood texture.

Red sandalwood chopsticks

Onmosia-henryi wooden chopsticks

Ironwood chopsticks

Date wood chopsticks

(2) Metal chopsticks

Nowadays, very few people use metal chopsticks to eat meals, but it was very popular for rich families in ancient times. The earliest metal chopsticks were bronze ones. Besides the bronze chopsticks of the Spring and Autumn Period unearthed in Guichi of Anhui Province, some bronze

Two pairs of copper chopsticks

chopsticks have also been excavated in Anyang, Henan Province.

"Copper chopsticks" died out chiefly because they produced toxicity from oxidization. Li Shizhen, a pharmacist of the Ming Dynasty (1368-1644), pointed out that copper utensils for drinks and tea would get toxic overnight and would harm one's voice if he or she drank medicine contained in copper utensils. People in later dynasties continued to use them but only to stoke the fire of the stove, or to

Twisted silver chopsticks

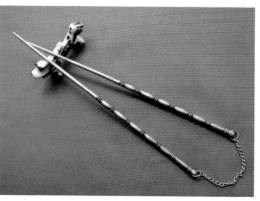

Bamboo and silver chopsticks

lengthen the candlewick for brighter lighting.

"Silver chopsticks" were the favorites for thousands of years, mainly because people deemed that they could discover toxicity in food, and besides they were durable and attractive. In fact, the use of silver in testing toxicity is not reliable. Silver chopsticks will lose brightness and turn dark only when contacted with arsenic or potassium cyanide. Some poisons do not produce sulfide and so silver chopsticks will not turn dark even if they are in them for a long time.

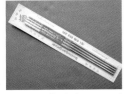
Stainless steel chopsticks

Aluminum chopsticks

"Gold chopsticks" were very expensive, meant only for emperors. Even officials could not afford them. The imperial palace once displayed the gold chopsticks that Empress Dowager of the Qing Dynasty used and they still kept their radiance though they were over a hundred years old. Also on display were jade chopsticks with gold mosaic and hexagonal ivory chopsticks with gold mosaic. These imperial chopsticks have great value in craftsmanship as antiques as well as symbols of the imperial supremacy of the emperors. In the late Qing Dynasty and early 20th century, gold chopsticks were no longer exclusive to the imperial family. Real estate tycoons, and Huang Jingrong and Du Yuesheng, gangsters, from Shanghai, had gold table decorations, namely, 10 gold wineglasses, 10 gold saucers,

Two pairs of iron chopsticks

10 pairs of gold chopsticks and 10 gold chopstick rests.

Metal chopsticks also include aluminum, stainless steel and alloy chopsticks, which are modern products.

(3) Ivory and bone chopsticks

Since the first ivory chopsticks of Emperor Zhou of the Shang Dynasty, the common folks regarded them as precious as pearl. In the classic story *Dream of the Red Mansions*, there was an episode about Granny Liu trying to use a pair of square ivory chopsticks to pick up cooked pigeon eggs. Because they were slippery the eggs fell off the chopsticks. The author's intention was to say that common folks could not afford ivory chopsticks and thus they were clumsy with them.

Patterns or characters could be engraved on ivory chopsticks. Years ago, at a curio shop in Shanghai I saw ten pairs of ivory chopsticks carved with pictures of birds and flowers. The bird's gestures and movements were lively and adorable while flowers were blooming in their

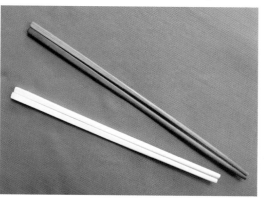

Old and new ivory chopsticks

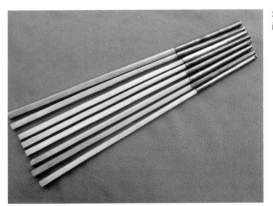

Silver-veneered ivory chopsticks

full beauty. Each of the ten pairs itself had its own picture. I really appreciated each pair of them, "parrot in red plum", "magpie with orchid", "ducks in lotus flowers" ⋯ They were indeed incredible. The only pity was that when I collected enough money to buy them the next day, they were already sold.

In recent years, because it is forbidden to hunt elephants the world over, ivory chopsticks have disappeared from dining tables, but of course they became favorites in antique markets.

Camel bone chopsticks

"Animal bone chopsticks" are easily distinguishable from ivory chopsticks by the informed though they look very similar. Animal bone chopsticks are mainly made of cattle bones, elephant bones, camel bones and occasionally deer bones. Patterns or Chinese characters are often carved on bone chopsticks.

Dragon horn chopsticks

Hawksbill chopsticks, made from turtle shell, are very rare and valuable. The chopsticks are interspersed with light brown and

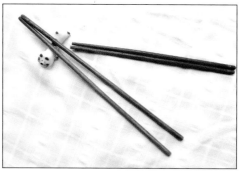

Red-dyed bone chopsticks

yellowish colors; they are bright and transparent.

"Jade chop-sticks" are always the favorites, since the Chinese people especially like jade. As early as the Neolithic Age some 7,000 to 8,000 years ago, Chinese ancestors started to make jade wares. Jade glasses, jade wine vessels and jade dragons are common archaeological findings of the Qin and Han dynasties, but jade chopsticks have been very rare.

The imperial kitchen of the Tang, Song, Yuan, Ming and Qing dynasties could not do without jade chopsticks because emperors liked to use them, for loving jade was an ancient tradition.

The fact that emperors liked jade chopsticks gave the imperial craftsmen a hard time. Once when Empress Dowager Cixi used em-

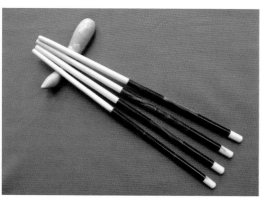

Ivory chopsticks

erald chopsticks she accidentally broke one. This was probably because of her long fingernails that prevented her from using chopsticks properly. Superstitious as she was, Empress Dowager Cixi flew off the handle and wanted to execute the eunuch in charge of chopsticks. Upon petition by many others his punishment was reduced to thirty floggings instead. Craftsmen, fearing that someone may lose their life, thought up, that very night, a way to solve the problem by using gold rings to hold the chopsticks. The chopsticks would be both reinforced and also marvelously elegant.

White jade chopsticks

Sapphire chopsticks

Dark jade chopsticks

Many kinds of jade are good materials for making chopsticks and turquoise is among the better ones. China is rich in reserves of turquoise of good quality and lush green color.

Coral, though not exactly a kind of mineral, has been broadly classified into the category of jade and stone since ancient times. Most coral chopsticks are red in color but many of those seen at antique markets are fakes made of animal bone and dyed with red color. There are very few coral chopsticks, which make them extremely valuable.

Turquoise chopsticks

Xiu-jade chopsticks

"Plastic chopsticks" whose dense

Ivory-imitation plastic chopsticks

amine bears the feature of ordinary plastics, are acid-proof, oil-proof and heat-resistance. They carry the color of porcelain and are hard instead of being brittle. Plastic chopsticks are ideal dining wares for modern times.

Porcelain chopsticks of earlier years, such as blue and white chopsticks, matching the colorful bowls and plates at the dining table, could only be listed as handicrafts without any practical value, because of their fragility.

Multi-colored plastic chopstick

Old celluloid chopsticks

Chinese Folk Customs and Chopsticks

Any country or nation has its own customs. China is a country of rites that stem from thousands of years ago with many complicated ceremonial formalities. Now many of the old rites are gradually dying out, but at the dining table, the elders continue to remind the younger generation of the "ten don'ts in using chopsticks".

The Han Chinese people have certain etiquette for using chopsticks. When guests are seated, they should not use or set their hands on the chopsticks before the host says to start. It is deemed impolite for one to pick up the chopsticks beforehand. After finishing the meal, guests should first place the chopsticks on the bowl to show that they are still respectfully accompanying the host at dinner. Only when the host puts down the chopsticks on the table, may guests move the chopsticks down from their bowl to the table, and then leave the seat. In regions of ethnic minority groups, the etiquette is different from the Han ethnic group. For example, in the mountainous villages of the Dong people in Guangxi Zhuang Autonomous Region, the host has to wait for the guest to start.

At the dining table, one should not reach out with the chopsticks over plates for dishes on the far side. When scholar Wang Anshi was said to take roe deer chest meat as his favorite,

his wife was puzzled because she knew Wang was never choosy about food. She discovered later, Wang, observing the etiquette of chopsticks, just took the deer chest meat that was nearest to him and never reached out for food on the far side. Now we have lazy Susan's to avoid the problem of reaching over too far.

The etiquette on chopsticks in the imperial court was different from that of the common folks. In his book, Xu Zhen of the Ming Dynasty told this story. Scholar Tang Su lost his officialdom and returned to his hometown. Emperor Zhu Yuanzhang liked and wanted to use his talent, and so he summoned him back and invited him to a dinner at the imperial palace. After the dinner, the scholar placed the chopsticks across in front of him. The emperor asked why was that. He answered that this was the etiquette of the common folks he learned when he was young. The emperor was furious and said how the etiquette of common folks could be used with the emperor. The scholar was thus punished and sent to be a guard at Haozhou. In fact, there was nothing wrong with placing chopsticks across the bowl. For the common folks, it was out of respect to the aged and older generations. But the emperor was outraged seeing common folks etiquette being observed at his court. Tang Su's problem was that he misjudged the temperament of the emperor.

For imperial banquets during the Qing Dynasty there were regulations that different classes used different dining wares. In 1796, Emperor Qianlong held a banquet in honor of a thousand aged men. The tables were divided into two classes. The first class was for the imperial families and relatives, officials of the top two ranks, and foreign envoys. The hot pot was made of silver and the chopsticks were square ebony ones. The second class was for the next seven official ranks. The hot pot was made of copper and chopsticks were ebony but cylindrical ones and a bit shorter than the square ones.

Chopsticks were not only dining tools but could also be seen as an auspicious omen in

some regions. On the wedding night in Yangzhou, Jiangsu Province, there was the custom of striking chopsticks and spreading chopsticks on the wedding bed. To celebrate the wedding, guests would walk into the bridal chamber holding a plate of red chopsticks and bowls. The leader, thrusting at the bottom of a bowl with chopsticks, shouted, "Chopsticks and chopsticks, have baby fast." (In Chinese, the term chopsticks is homonym to the expression of having a baby boy very soon—translator) After everybody answered yeah, he continued, "Chopsticks are round at one end and square at the other, and the baby will become a manager after he grows up." Thrusting the bottom of a bowl with chopsticks indicated the act of making love. Then everybody would spread boundless new chopsticks on the wedding bed while singing verses like, "Chopsticks, chopsticks, have baby fast", "Spreading chopsticks will bring sons and grandsons, a full house", "Spreading chopsticks on the bed will bring rice and a full granary."

At wedding ceremonies in old times, the bride's head was covered with a piece of red cloth. In Qidong, Hunan, upon the bride entering the wedding chamber, the bridegroom was not allowed to take off the red cloth but the mother-in-law would use chopsticks to lift it off, implying the chopsticks would help to produce a baby fast.

There are many interesting customs in the wedding ceremonies of ethnic minorities. At the wedding of the She people in Zhejiang Province, the bridegroom will see nothing at the table upon his entering the bride's home. This is not meant to give the groom the cold shoulder but rather to test his singing ability. Upon singing songs about drinks and dishes the groom will be given drinks and dishes. He will then sing, "Wedding banquet should have chopsticks. Only a pair of chopsticks will help pick the food. When I have chopsticks, I will have baby fast. The bridegroom is coming to take the bride." On this occasion, the groom will not be able to take home the bride if he does not sing.

The wedding ceremony of Tujia people in Hubei Province was focused on the "Crying Wedding" song. If the bride could not sing "Crying Wedding" she would not be allowed to get onto the sedan. So girls of the Tujia people, at the age of 12 or 13 would be taught by their mothers to sing the song. There were ten verses. The major one was "crying while spreading chopsticks". When the bride was spreading chopsticks around the sedan, she would be singing and crying, "A torch lights

up, a bundle of chopsticks of 12 pairs. Chopsticks are in pairs and I match my groom. I am getting married and spreading chopsticks far and wide. My elder brother picks chopsticks to enjoy happiness; my younger brother picks chopsticks to keep them in a box; my younger sister picks chopsticks to find her man; my cousin picks chopsticks and she will laugh and sing. They will have good luck all their lives." The content of the song is very rich but the theme is centered on the compassionate feeling of departure as she gives her best wishes to her parents, brothers and sisters by spreading chopsticks.

Weddings of girls of the Achang people in Yunnan Province are full of laughter. When the groom goes to the bride's home her father will prepare breakfast for him. On the table are soft bean curd, fine starch  noodles and fried peanuts. The father will give the groom a pair of one-meter-long, thin bamboo chopsticks with bamboo leaves at one end, which are newly cut bamboo shoots. The chopsticks are very difficult to handle. As the groom shows his awkwardness with the large chopsticks, the guests burst into laughter. The groom must try by all means possible to get some food into his mouth. This is to remind the groom that happiness does not come along easily.

Weddings of the Yi people in Yunnan Province have their own customs with regards to chopsticks. Sisters of the bride, at her request, specially make chopsticks with dragons' heads and flowers for the bridegroom. Two little dragons made of thin wires have two silk flowers on their horns and tails. They are fastened onto the top of the chopsticks. The dragon-head chopsticks are inserted standing upright into the dish prepared by the bride. When the groom comes to the banquet, male and female guests will make fun of the groom, such as putting ashes onto his face. Whatever they do, they should be careful to avoid knocking down or damaging the chopsticks with dragonhead and flower decorations, because they symbolize the unbreakable love between the bride and the groom.

After the wedding of the Lisu people, the bridegroom and the bride will exchange chopsticks and bowls. The legend says that the exchange of chopsticks and bowls means the exchange of hearts and the new couple will live in harmony for the rest of their lives.

The proposal of marriage among Gelao people in Guizhou Province is unique. Upon learning that their son has set his sights on a girl, the parents would wrap up a pair of new chopsticks with a piece of red paper. When they get to the girls' home, they will respectfully put it on the table in the living room and then leave without saying a word. When the parents of the girl open it they know it is a wedding proposal as soon as they see the pair of chopsticks.

At weddings of the Mongolians on the grassland, the most beautiful part is the chopsticks dance. There is no special organization or formality. After the dinner, people in high spirits and with a bundle of chopsticks come out of the tent and dance around the flaming bonfire. They use chopsticks to beat their shoulders and thighs with rhythms.

In the old days, chopsticks were used in different ways in the hope of conception and smooth births. In 1854, Courtesan Yibin (later known Empress Dowager Cixi) became pregnant. Hoping for a smooth delivery, she ordered a eunuch to dig a lucky hole to bury chopsticks, red silk cloth, gold and silver and other things at a pre-selected place of good omen. This kind of imperial custom spread to the common folks, who began to follow suit. In the region south of the Yangtze River, there is the custom of ensuring smooth and fast delivery of babies involving chopsticks. When the woman is several months pregnant, her mother would send her chopsticks, ginger and rice because they share similar pronunciation to fast delivery of precious baby. There are other similar customs: to put a pair of chopsticks in the cradle for the baby; to put or hide chopsticks under the pillow of a recently married or pregnant woman; to lightly tap sterile women with chopsticks.

Though chopsticks are small, they follow the life of the people from marriage to conception, to delivery. They also follow to the funeral customs. Various kinds of chopsticks unearthed from the tombs of different dynasties show that China kept the traditional custom of burying chopsticks with the deceased for thousands of years. In the traditional funeral customs of the Han people, there was the offering of a meal for the deceased. The chopsticks were not laid flat on the table but inserted upright in the middle of the bowl. In order to keep the chopsticks standing firmly, rice was piled up to the brim of the rice bowl. A common custom of the Han people was that when a person over seventy

Little hawksbill chopsticks with silver chain of the Qing Dynasty

years old passed away, some friends or relatives of the deceased would "steal" chopsticks and bowls from the deceased family, which was called "stealing longevity".

This picture, done by Li Binsheng, is about using long hexagonal wooden chopsticks to eat roasted meat in Beijing in the 1930s. I once chatted with Mr. Deng Yunxiang, a folklorist, about hexagonal wood. The late Deng told me that hexagonal wood was a wild plant whose branches and twigs were long and straight. After peeling off the branch, there were six concave grains around it, thus it was named hexagonal wood. It was white and hard, making it a good material for long chopsticks and for eating roasted meat. Another interesting story about hexagonal wood relates to it being native to Laiyuan of Hebei Province at the foot of the Great Wall. According to the legend, hexagonal wood in the Song Dynasty (960-1279) was called "harnessing dragon wood". General Yang's family borrowed the harnessing dragon wood to break a battle fortress. In 1993, I happened to read an article of hexagonal wood in the *Chinese Cultural Journal*, so I bought two pairs of hexagonal wood chopsticks from the author.

Stories about Chopsticks

For thousands of years, chopsticks have been a daily tool in the life of the Chinese people, and every family, rich or poor, has chopsticks, more or less, ordinary and extraordinary. Every Chinese person, from childhood to advanced age, could not live without them for a single day. People use chopsticks at meals. On some occasions, they use them to predict the future, or use them as a pen, things of trust, or even as a weapon for murder. There are historical records as well as folktales about chopsticks.

As early as in the Tang Dynasty (618-907), Vietnam and other countries started to use chopsticks. Chopsticks were introduced to Japan after the Tang Dynasty period. Japanese people like and respect chopsticks as much as the Chinese people. To express their gratitude to chopsticks for their hard work every day, the Japanese people declared the 4th of August as the "Chopsticks Day". In Japan, chopsticks are usually shorter and sharp at the lower end. They are divided into different categories, like vegetable chopsticks and fish chopsticks for cooking, painted chopsticks and disposable chopsticks for eating meals. Disposable chopsticks are for guests to use and then discard them after the meal. More than a dozen years ago, disposable chopsticks were introduced into China and became popular in restaurants all over.

Ricci Matteo (1552-1610), an Italian, was among the first to introduce Chinese chopsticks into Europe. In his *Notes on China*, he described chopsticks. Over many years, China has increased its exchanges with foreign countries, and chopsticks, along with Chinese cuisine have been included. Many foreigners can skilfully use chopsticks. Some even did research to invent automatic chopsticks with spring devices, or chips for computerized chopsticks, so as to meet the needs of those who like Chinese food but could not use chopsticks.

To be frank, to get Westerners who are used to a knife and a fork, to use chopsticks is no easy matter. Occasionally, interesting episodes about chopsticks from state banquets or family dinners occur.

Stirring up trouble with chopsticks

Emperor Jing of the Han Dynasty was not on good terms with Zhou Yafu, his Prime Minister he inherited from the previous emperor. After taking the throne, the emperor was angry with Zhou because the latter opposed the appointment of imperial relatives as dukes. Emperor Jing was waiting for opportunities to fix Zhou by making use of chopsticks. One day, the emperor invited Zhou to dinner but at the table, there were only big chunks of meat. There were no chopsticks at the table, a deliberate trap for Zhou. Zhou was not happy about it and left his seat to pick up chopsticks. Emperor Jing took this opportunity to reproach Zhou for not behaving like a gentleman, and later criticized his action as inferior to that of a prime minister. Zhou Yafu could not eat anything for five days and in the end he vomited blood and died.

To refuse marriage by breaking a chopstick

In the Tang Dynasty, Yu Chong, a scholar, won first place in the imperial examination. Emperor Xuanzong decided to marry his daughter Princess Yongfu to him. The princess was not willing to marry the scholar but found it hard to tell her father directly. So

when she was having dinner with the emperor, she deliberately broke one chopstick. Seeing one chopstick broken, the Emperor learned about his daughter's unwillingness to marry Yu Chong. Bad consequences might result if he forced the marriage. However, the emperor could not go back on his word, so he had to marry Princess Yongfu to Yu.

To draw lots to decide the prime minister

Emperor Mingzong of the Tang Dynasty (926-933) was not able to make up his mind on the appointment of the prime minister. One day, he, on sudden impulse, wrote the names of several ministers on chopsticks and put them in a porcelain jar. He then shook the jar until one of the chopsticks fell out of the jar and onto the ground. The person, whose name was on this chopstick, would be the prime minister. As a result, a minister named Lu Jiwen was absurdly appointed the post.

To test with chopsticks

Liu Bowen, a high official who helped the first emperor of the Ming Dynasty Zhu Yuanzhang to found the dynasty, was a learned and intelligent man. It was a small chopstick that bound Liu Bowen and Emperor Zhu together. It was said that when Liu first met the emperor, the sovereign ruler was having a meal with chopsticks in his hand. So he asked Liu to make couplets on chopsticks. Seeing the emperor holding Xiang courtesan bam-

boo chopsticks, Liu voiced out two verses, "A couple of jade stones stand shoulder to shoulder on the Xiang River, two courtesans left their tear traces on them." Hearing these two verses, the emperor knew Liu was talking about the story of Erhuang and Nuying crying over the death of Emperor Shun. However, the emperor regarded Liu as too bookish. Hearing this, Liu mouthed out another two verses, "Four hundred years of Han Dynasty reign were determined by the borrowing of chopsticks by Zhang Liang." It was about how Zhang Liang borrowed chopsticks to stop the erroneous decision by the drunkard Li Sheng and helped Emperor Liu Bang to turn over the tide to eventually found the Han Dynasty.

Through testing Liu Bowen on poems about chopsticks, the emperor hoped that Liu would help him to accomplish the founding of the Ming Dynasty just like Zhang Liang helped his sovereign ruler Liu Bang. In later years, Liu Bowen indeed became military adviser to the would-be Ming emperor and helped him to take the throne as the first sovereign ruler of the Ming Dynasty.

Collection of chopsticks by a treacherous prime minister

Yan Song, a treacherous prime minister of the Ming Dynasty, was dismissed and sentenced to prison at an advanced age for his crime of corruption and embezzlement. When his house was searched, a total of 27,159 pairs of chopsticks were confiscated. These included 2 pairs of gold chopsticks, 1,110 pairs of gold-veneered ivory chopsticks, 10 pairs of hawksbill chopsticks, 2,691 pairs of ivory chopsticks, 5,931 pairs of Xiang courtesan bamboo chopsticks, 1,009 pairs of silver-mosaic ivory chopsticks, 6,896 pairs of ebony wood chopsticks and 9,510 pairs of painted chopsticks. Yan was the largest collector of chopsticks in three thousand years but he did not collect chopsticks to appreciate their beauty and was only a corrupted official who lived a debauched and decadent life.

To use chopsticks as a pen

It was said that when Emperor Qianlong of the Qing Dynasty inspected the south, he got to the bank of Taihu Lake near Suzhou. It

was too late and he had to put up for the night in the boat of a fisherman. The emperor was already hungry while an old lady was still preparing food. The emperor started to taste the shredded eel and fresh shrimps, which he called "dragon swims among coins". After he finished the dish, the emperor wanted more, but the lady started to cry. She told the emperor that her son caught the eel and shrimp in the morning but in the afternoon the son was put into prison by the county magistrate for his refusal to give contributions. The old lady was worried about their future life. Hearing the story of the fisherman and his mother, the emperor promised to write a letter, which could get her son out of prison. There was no ink or pen in the boat, but the emperor had a good idea. He used chopsticks as the pen and fire-ashes with water as the ink. He wrote, "Chopsticks were used as the pen and fire-ashes as the ink. What crime had the old lady's son committed? Reunion of the mother and son would help catch fish and shrimps. Delicious dishes prepared by the lady make the emperor happy." The county magistrate was scared to death and kneeled down to beg for pardon when the eunuch showed him the letter written with chopsticks.

The case of the willow chopsticks murder

In the years under the reign of Emperor Qianlong, a county magistrate named Ma disguised as an ordinary man inspected villages.

One day as he passed Niujiagou Village he heard noises. The magistrate elbowed into the crowd to find a dead peasant lying on his back, at the edge of a field at the foot of a hill. Beside the dead body, there was a young lady screaming and crying. The magistrate learned that the dead man was named Liu Tieshan and the lady was his widow. The magistrate made a careful observation and investigation of the case. He noticed that the lady's cry was loud but not sad, high-pitched but not trembling. Suspecting that something must be fishy, he chatted with the folks around and learned that the peasant worked like an ox in the field in the morning till lunchtime when his wife came with food. Liu Tieshan opened the pot to find fragrant chicken with chestnuts. The delicious dish made two folks nearby mouth watering, so Liu gave them some chicken soup and handed them chops of chicken meat. At this moment, the lady complained that she had forgotten to bring chopsticks. She went to a willow tree and broke a branch off the tree. She then used an axe to cut the branch into two and gave her husband the makeshift chopsticks. Liu took the willow chopsticks and finished the chicken and rice in a minute. Then he went on to plough the field. As the wife cleaned the bowl and pot and threw away the willow chopsticks and got ready to go back home, she heard her husband suddenly scream in pain. Before he had taken ten steps on the plough, he could not stop vomiting. When his wife and the two folks rushed to his side, Liu was already dead on the edge of the field.

After initial investigation of the case, the magistrate ordered the widow be detained. In the meantime, he consulted with local doctors to analyze the case. They all felt the problem lay in the food. However, after examination of the chicken and chestnuts, there was found to be no poison in them. Moreover, the two folks who had the same food were perfectly all right. One old doctor said, when he was learning medicine many years ago, his teacher received a patient that was a similar case to Liu. He remembered the teacher said that chopsticks were the cause of death. Everybody present was shocked at this news. It turned out that willow chopsticks themselves were not poisonous, neither were the chicken and chestnuts. But the three could not go together. This is one of the prohibitions about serving certain foods.

Seeing a breakthrough in the case, the magistrate started to investigate. The widow at first did not admit her intention to murder her husband, but she had to confess when it was pointed out that she intentionally forgot to bring chopsticks. Ultimately it turned out that not long before, she had met and grew close with a doctor. The two had secretly plotted to murder her husband.

Diplomat Gu Weijun and chopsticks

Gu Weijun, a famous diplomat of early last

century, attended a dinner held by Yuan Shikai, the then president of China, in 1913. At the dinner in honor of Mongolian and Tibetan kings, Yuan, himself alone, sat at one table and six people sat at each of the other ten tables. Getting seated, Gu Weijun felt hungry. Seeing the glossy roasted duck on the table, he reached out his chopsticks for some duck meat. But he could not get anything out of the duck, so he thought something must be wrong with the chopsticks. When he lowered his head to take a careful look, he found it to be a painted wood duck. This was the usual trick that the dinner organizer used to embezzle money. Those sophisticated officials who often attended these occasions would never set their chopsticks on these kinds of ducks. But Gu Weijun who just came back from the United States did not know this, so it was unavoidable for him to become a laughing stock.

George Bernard Shaw and chopsticks

The famous Irish playwright George Bernard Shaw visited Shanghai in 1933. Soong Chingling, widow of Sun Yat-sen who served as the first president of the Republic of China after the overthrow of the feudal Qing Dynasty in 1911, held a dinner in his honor. Shaw declined the host's good intention of letting him use a knife and fork and insisted on using chopsticks. He was sweating while trying to pick up a meatball. He finally managed to lift one but it only fell off the chopsticks before he managed to bring it into his bowl. He consoled himself by saying, it must be made of rabbit meat, or it could not have run so quickly like a rabbit. This drew laughs from everybody. Then Shaw picked up the meatball with chopsticks and said, "If I had not learned to use chopsticks, how could the British people believe that I had visited China?"

Queen Elizabeth and chopsticks

When Queen Elizabeth II first visited China in October 1986, the BBC broadcast three special programs about her tour everyday. The British people were most keen on seeing how the Queen managed chopsticks at dinner in the Great Hall of the People. When many British people saw the Queen on TV adroitly use the chopsticks they could not help applauding. They might not know that before she visited China, to avoid the embarrassment of being unable to use chopsticks the queen practiced using chopsticks time and again, and sometimes she even had sore arms. *The Daily Telegraph* carried a huge close-up of a Chinese waiter preparing chopsticks for the queen. The special correspondent from *The Sun* used the queen picking longan with chopsticks as the headline to report the queen's attendance at the state banquet. Thanks to the simultaneous reports by several newspapers and magazines on the queen using chopsticks in Beijing, chopsticks became a hot topic in Great Britain.

Chopsticks Culture

During the long history of chopsticks, craftsmen, through their intelligence and creative work, made the technique and craftsmanship more and more perfect, making the practical tool of daily necessity an artistic charm and new culture.

Ancient chopsticks were mostly cylindrical and later developed into cylindrical in the lower part, and square in the upper part in the Ming Dynasty. The strongpoint was that they would not roll if put on the table, and also provided space for men of letters to show their talents by painting on the chopsticks. I have collected a pair of ivory chopsticks of the Ming Dynasty on which artists had carved a landscape of a house, bushes, single-sail boat and mountains far in the background, with an old man and a young man sitting facing each other. This vivid picture added great artistic value to the ordinary ivory chopsticks.

Earlier, I bought a pair of creamy ivory chopsticks and asked Mr. Huang Zhenghe, a micro-carving master artist, to carve the poem *Song of Bamboo Chopsticks* by Cheng Lianggui, a poet of the Ming Dynasty. Two verses were carved on each of the chopsticks displaying a graceful cutting technique.

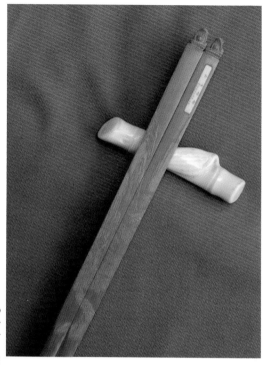

Long bamboo chopsticks engraved with landscape

Carvers can find better methods of expression with bamboo chopsticks. One of the most memorable pairs of bamboo chopsticks was made in a special way. The skin of the bamboo was completely peeled away leaving only the very inside part for making chopsticks. On the upper part of the chopsticks, mountain ridges were engraved, on the lower old pine trees with a pavilion in the middle of the mountain. This is among the best of bamboo chopsticks.

Artistic chopsticks can have carvings on one, two sides or all four sides. I have a collection of silver-mosaic bamboo chopsticks of the late Ming Dynasty. A four-verse poem was engraved on each side. A pair of simple bamboo chopsticks could never get into the hall of fame of literature. But once a well-known artist engraved it, its value increased by a hundred times and itself became an artistic work, which one would never tolerate being used at meals, no matter how delicious the food was.

In spring of 1998, I fortunately visited the curio market on Dongtai Road in Shanghai. There I set my eyes on eight pairs of silver-mosaic bamboo chopsticks of the Qing Dynasty with verses of a poem engraved on all four sides. I was appalled at the price 4,500 yuan for the lot or about 550 yuan per pair. The vendor claimed they were not expensive at all for ancient silver-mosaic chopsticks and at over 500 years old, they only averaged one yuan per year. I liked the eight pairs of chopsticks because each had a verse of poems engraved, not because of their age.

I checked many ancient books and cuisine newspapers and magazines and failed to find any more poems written on chopsticks except for a few by Cheng Lianggui of the Ming Dynasty. Now it seems the eight pairs of chopsticks were indeed a lucky gain of my many years' of painstaking efforts and searching in vain.

One poem (author unknown) from the pairs of chopsticks follows:

The shape of square upper and cylindrical lower is extolled.

Bamboo chopsticks engraved with poems on four sides, Ming Dynasty

The platform for a new dynasty, by their movement, is already told.

With a view to conservation of all of heaven and earth,

You're advised not to have them disposed.

Perhaps chopsticks are things of daily necessity that cannot reach the heights of elite literature. Men of letters and poets seldom wrote about chopsticks but in comparison, common folks were more compassionate. Nevertheless, a couple of famous poets left some poems about chopsticks for history.

Yuan Mu, a scholar of the Qing Dynasty, wrote the poem *Song of Chopsticks:*

It is ironic you are busy with seizing,
Into the mouth of others you are sending.
Your life is full of salt and sour,

Could you discern the taste at all?

Some critics commented that Yuan Mu wrote this poem to complain of his whole life of unhappy officialdom. Yuan was not only a poet but also a gastronome. At the age of forty he retired to go back to Nanjing to set up the Sui Garden and to make friends. There he lived a leisurely life. At the age of seventy-three, he finished the world famous cooking book, *Menu of the Sui Garden*. In his decades in the Sui Garden where he tasted the menus of many family restaurants, Yuan had a special feeling towards chopsticks, so he wrote the following light poem on chopsticks:

> Like two ladies small and thin,
> Their waists are held to open the feet.
> To taste the flavors, good or bad,
> You have to reach out the tongue to feed.

Zhu Shuzhen, a female poet of the Song Dynasty, wrote a poem on chopsticks like a riddle. Some critics doubted that it was her poem because it lacked the literature of ancient poems. But some others disagreed by saying that she wrote the poem to vex her depressed feeling by composing *To Chopsticks:*

> Diligence questioned chopsticks,
> You first taste bitter or sweet.
> Others get good flavor happily,
> You reap nothing with busy feet.

Mr. Feng Jicai, vice chairman of the Chinese Writers Association, wrote a better poem on chopsticks that he mailed to me:

Do not allege chopsticks are small,
Daily meals they accompany you all.
The history of bitter and sweet,
Only chopsticks can fully tell.

Since ancient times, among the common folks there have been many riddles concerning chopsticks because they are closest to people's everyday life, three times daily, at each meal. For example, twin brothers, with long and thin bodies, like dishes rather than soup. Another example, with little round feet and square head, they come in and out in pairs. They are caught twice or three times in the day and at night they are punished to stand until daybreak. Riddles of the common folks are simple with humorous language.

There are also compassionate and sad personified riddles:

The bodies are thin and seven inches long.
They are cut off from their mountainous
homeland.
They suffer in hot oil and boiling water.
They could never see their mother.

There are also riddles to belittle chopsticks. One example: Twin brothers are the same height. They come out but never talk. At meal times they are the first to appear. At work time they never show up.

Wherever there are chopsticks in China there are popular riddles about them. The following are some examples.

There is a bundle of chives in the kitchen.
They will all be pulled out when guests come.

Twin sisters go to the dining table, they come and go between spice and sauce, and bathe in hot water.

Two babies are the same height, thin and small. They will be first to taste the delicious food but will never put on weight and grow up.

Besides engraving, there are techniques like mosaic, mother-of-pearl, wire inlay and pyrography. Take ivory chopsticks for example. The ivory chopsticks as the main body may have the middle part inlaid with green dragon horn. So the chopsticks are white with harmonious green. The Miao people take ox-horn as the main body for chopsticks, which are inset with ivory on the top and bottom.

There are many ways of using mother-of-pearl, for instance, to inlay in shell or hardwood. Wire inlay is a cloisonné technique for chopsticks and because they are so thin, they are more difficult to work on. Pyrography is a traditional technique. In the Qing Dynasty, a Mr. Wu Tian in Yunnan Province could im-print landscape, portraits, flowers and birds on bamboo chopsticks. A talented craftsman, Mr. Wu was a constant drunkard. Poor as he was, he was often invited by his neighbors to have a drink. They would place new chopsticks and dishes near the stove and as he took a drop too much, he started to burn imprints of birds, animals or flowers on chopsticks, at an extremely quick speed.

Chopstick Holders, Rests and Boxes

A bamboo chopstick holder with 21 chopsticks and a painted spoon in it was unearthed in No. 167 Tomb of the Han Dynasty in Jiangling. A bamboo chopstick holder with 16 bamboo chopsticks was found in a tomb of the Han Dynasty in Yunmeng of Hubei Province. There were bamboo chopstick holders as early as in the Han Dynasty (206 BC-AD 220).

The following is a brief introduction of chopstick holders some eighty years ago, which showed the customs or history of the time. Chopsticks holder may fall into the following six categories, namely pottery, porcelain, bamboo, wood, brick and metal.

(1) Pottery chopstick holders

Pottery holders of the late Qing Dynasty were mostly half-glazed, only the surface but not the bottom was glazed.

Chopstick holder with characters meaning good fortune, happiness, longevity, a hundred sons and a thousand grandsons.

Glazed chopstick holder with the characters of a hundred sons and a thousand grandsons

百子千孫

Cicada-shaped chopstick holder of the Qing Dynasty

Chopstick holder with the characters of bumper harvest

Green-glazed holders had "a hundred sons and a thousand grandsons" on the rim of the holder. China was an agricultural country and more sons and grandsons meant more labor power. Therefore, chopsticks and chopstick holders became a symbol of a thriving family. Another pottery holder had a couplet engraved, "This holder holds a thousand chopsticks; the family houses five hundred people".

A cicada-shaped chopstick holder of the Qing Dynasty was made of clay and looked rough but vivid just like a cicada on a tree, when it was hung on the wooden pillar in the kitchen.

Chopstick holders with characters meaning "The people's commune is fine."

In the 1950s, farmers were still using pottery chopstick holders but "hundred sons and thousand grandsons" was replaced by "bumper harvest" and "people's commune is fine" and patterns of fortune, happiness and longevity were replaced by patterns of wheat and rice ears.

Pottery chopstick holders with illustrations of workers, peasants and soldiers studying *Selected Works of Mao Zedong* were products of the Cultural Revolution (1966-76). It is now thirty years since then and these kinds of holders have become collector's items, if not historic relics.

Chopstick holder with "workers, farmers and soldiers studying *Selected Works of Mao Zedong*"

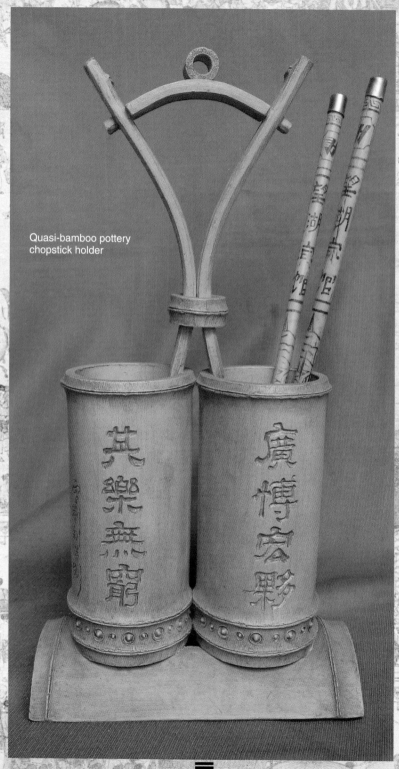

Quasi-bamboo pottery
chopstick holder

(2) Porcelain chopstick holders

The difference of porcelain holders from pottery holders is that the former is fully glazed with fine workmanship and beautiful patterns, so the price is higher. In the past, only rich families in the cities used porcelain holders while the poor used pottery and brick holders.

Chopstick holders with patterns of three green vegetable leaves on the top, and white stems at the bottom, were popular during the Qing Dynasty. They were hung in the kitchen to create a garden

Fish-shaped chopstick holder of the Qing Dynasty

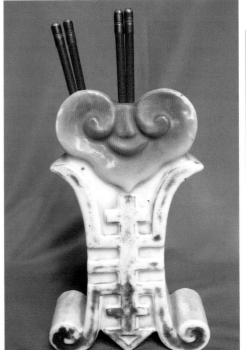

Vegetable-shaped chopstick holder of the Qing Dynasty

Porcelain chopstick holder with the character for rice

Blue and white porcelain chopstick holder with the pattern of water birds

Chopstick holder with the pattern of a boy herding cattle

Fan-shaped porcelain chopstick holder

atmosphere.

A fish-shaped chopstick holder of the Qing Dynasty was unique. The fish had a big head with a big open mouth serving as the holder's mouth.

A porcelain chopstick holder from the era of Emperor Guangxu of the Qing Dynasty had a pattern of chrysanthemums at the front and at the back it had the following characters "the sixth year of Guangxu, for

Porcelain chopstick holders with the chrysanthemum pattern

A chopstick holder with a lady design

Xiong Laxiang". This was certainly made by a folk kiln but for a rich man named Xiong Laxiang, and the year was 1880.

(3) Bamboo chopstick holders

Southern China is rich in bamboo. The simplest one is made by just sawing off a section of bamboo and punching a hole at the back to hang it on the wall. It is conveniently placed on the table.

Bamboo chopstick holders with fish pattern engraved on a peeled bamboo surface is simple but with some artistic value.

Twin bamboo chopstick holders: The making of chopstick holders with bamboo does not need any nails or glue. The two are bound together with bamboo slices and sticks.

Twin bamboo chopstick holders

Shoe-shaped bamboo chopstick holder

Bamboo chopstick holder engraved with fish pattern

(4) Wooden chopstick holders

The first time I saw a wooden chopstick holder was twenty years ago when I visited Chairman Mao's former residence in Shaoshan, Hunan Province. On the wall of the kitchen, a long square wooden chopstick holder left a deep impression on me. Hunan Province has many forests and mountains. Farmers in the mountainous villages can easily cut trees to make wooden chopstick holders.

Wooden chopstick holder with the character of filial piety

A red sandalwood chopstick holder with depictions of a unicorn is quite different from the ordinary wooden holders of the farmers in Hunan. The holder had fine and vivid carvings of a unicorn and a crane. It was not only

Red sandalwood chop-
stick holder with the pattern of a unicorn

a chopstick holder but also an elegant work of art.

A wooden chopstick holder with the Chinese character meaning "filial piety" was a special chopstick holder for the occasion of a funereal dinner by rich families. In the past when an elder died, his or her children had to observe the rites of filial piety for three years. The family had to change to using white mulberry-wood chopstick holders to treat guests for meals and such a holder should be engraved with the character meaning "filial piety".

(5) Brick chopstick holders

They were made of clay then baked in a kiln. Characters or patterns would be engraved on the holder before or after they were baked.

Brick chopstick holder with characters of "Don't forget national humiliation": Around 1915, Yuan Shikai, betraying the nation, signed a humiliating treaty of twenty-one clauses with the Japanese. Workers, businessmen and students throughout the whole country took the streets to demonstrate and protest against Yuan. This brick holder, though looking earthy, is a witness and product of the awareness and the patriotism of the nation in those days.

Brick chopstick holder engraved with a pattern of twin fish is rich with rustic charm. This holder which has a simple cut of two fish looks

Chopstick holder engraved with the characters of "don't forget national humiliation"

Fretted chopstick holder

Twin fish chopstick holder

Red brick chopstick holder with longevity and chopstick holder with the characters of happiness, chrysanthemum chopsticks holder

more ancient and rough and primitive in style.

Red brick chopstick holder of longevity is different from most brick holders, which are either grey or black. In early 1910, foreign red brick houses were built in China. Brick-makers learned this Western style and baked red brick chopstick holders from red clay but they were only made in small quantities.

Patterns on small and simple brick chopstick holders boomed with varieties, birds, flowers, calligraphy of good omen, so on and so forth, to the tastes and likes of everyone.

(6) Metal chopstick holders

They could rarely be found in ordinary families. In ancient times, metal products were expensive, so common folks could not afford them. Moreover, metal chopstick holders became rusty easily because wet chopsticks would bring or drip water into the holders. I only have one example of a copper chopstick holder, which is about a hundred years old.

Patterns on small and simple brick chopstick holders boomed with varieties

Brick chopstick holder with the pattern of "East is red."

Chopstick companions also include chopstick rests and chopstick boxes. Chopstick rests are also referred to as chopstick pillows.

The first chopstick rests of my collection are a pair of colorful baby-shaped chopstick rests. The babies are crawling down on the ground with raised heads and feet and their lowered waists are just right for resting

Colorful baby-shaped chopstick rests.

chopsticks. Added later to my collection were fish-shaped jade chopstick rests, which matched jade chopsticks perfectly. Chopstick rests were not limited to that though. Once I bought twelve pairs of bamboo chopsticks carved with designs of the twelve animals of the Chinese zodiac and I wanted to match them with chopstick rests. In Changsha, I saw artistic decorative ornaments of little animals of the Chinese zodiac. As a matter of fact, they were porcelain toys rather than chopstick rests, but they matched perfectly with my bamboo chopsticks. Enlightened by the idea, I also bought little ornaments of cucumbers, peppers and other vegetables to serve as chopstick rests.

Copper chopstick rests could hold chopsticks and spoons, and some with a hole in the middle could hold toothpicks. I have a collection of a silver-plated copper chopsticks rest, a product of the 1930s. It has the characters of Golden Gate Hotel engraved on it.

Chopstick boxes are mainly made of hardwood. There are different kinds of chopstick boxes, such as a box for one pair, for two pairs or for five pairs. Boxes for one or two

Copper chopstick rest of the Qing Dynasty and Golden Gate Hotel chopstick rest

pairs usually slide open. Hardwood chopstick boxes inlaid with silver threads are of better quality. The box for two pairs of chopsticks with Chinese characters meaning flying shoulder to shoulder is an ideal gift for the newlyweds.

Blue and white porcelain chopstick rests.

Boxes for five pairs of chopsticks usually flip open from the top. Engraved on the front are patterns of pine trees and cranes or five little turtles, which stand for longevity. These boxes are good gifts for the aged.

A chopstick box with Chinese characters saying "Memory of the China Events" is a shocking relic. In 1937, Japan started aggression against China and on the 13th of August it occupied Shanghai. Some Japanese living in Shanghai engraved those characters in memory of the so-called Japanese victory. Eight years later the defeated Japanese army surrendered and returned to Japan, leaving this box behind. The box, a witness of the crime of Japanese aggression, was found in a junk market.

All in all, either chopstick holders, or chopstick rests or chopstick boxes are full of stories of Chinese traditional culture and customs of the past several thousand years.

Hardwood chopstick box

Conservation and Appreciation of Chopsticks

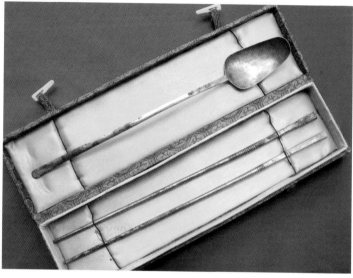

Gilded silver chopsticks of the Tang Dynasty. Silver spoon with long handle.

The silver chopsticks are 28 centimeters long, square on the upper part and cylindrical at the bottom part. At around 7 centimeters from the top, there is a gilded ring ornament. They were buried underground for thousands of years but it is easy to distinguish the gold from the silver. The silver spoon is 27.2 centimeters long, with 20 centimeters of handle and 7.2 centimeters of spoon. The ancient chopsticks and spoon, over a thousand years old, were excavated at the same time.

The chopsticks are relatively short, only 21 centimeters. They are cylindrical with the thick top and become thin down lower. The chopsticks used to be sky-blue and have faded over the years.

This pair of chopsticks (below) are 27.7 centimeters long with a 2-centimeter- long silver cover inlaid on the top and a 10.5 centimeters silver chain linking the pair together. The bottom part has a 7.5-centimeter-long silver cover.

Turquoise chopsticks of the Song Dynasty

The chopsticks (next page) are 28 centimeters long engraved with poetic verses and

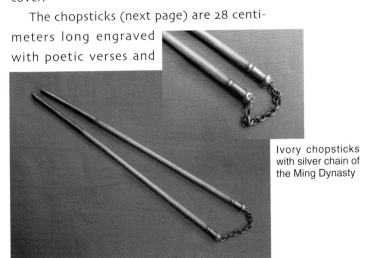

Ivory chopsticks with silver chain of the Ming Dynasty

Ivory chopsticks of the
Ming Dynasty

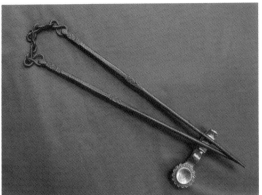

Copper chopsticks of the Ming Dynasty used for bonfire

landscape. The details could only be seen via magnifying glasses because the carving lines are as thin as hair. At the riverside and with mountain ridges far behind, an old man and a young man are sitting in the forests. What are they talking about? It lies in the two poetic verses on top; "It is nice to watch the river on a spring day. The two sitting by rocks are reciting poems together."

They (below) are 20 centimeters long. The top silver lids can be flipped open, a 5-centimeter-long silver toothpick is hidden inside

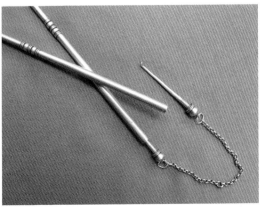

Silver chopsticks of the Ming Dynasty

one and a silver ear-pick in the other.

Dragon horn (below), also known as walrus tusk, is often dyed to make chopsticks. The chopsticks (below) are 23.5 centimeters long, and on the top, a 1.5- centimeter crown-shaped gold lid was inlaid, in addition to a 1.2- centimeter gold ring in the middle and a 6.8-centimeter gold cover on the bottom.

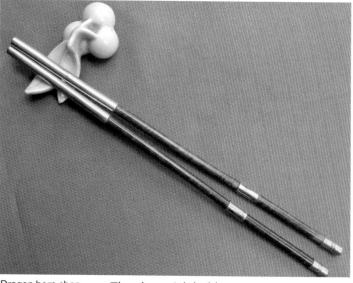

Dragon horn chopsticks of the Qing Dynasty

The chopstick holder (next page), 34 centimeters in length, is made of wood veneered with sharkskin. Its both ends have copper covers, which can flip open. At the bigger end, there are hidden two pairs of chopsticks, two forks, a knife, an ivory toothpick and an iron clip, and two spoons (one with sieve to pick vegetables and the other for soup). At the smaller end, there were hidden two silver wineglasses and two silver saucers. The marvelous part of the holder is that each tool has

Wood chopstick holder veneered with sharkskin of the Qing Dynasty

its own fixed place. Once everything is in place, one may close the copper lids and hang it on the saddle. It will not be damaged or lost. This used to serve as compact dining tools for the Mongolian and Manchu kings and generals of the Qing Dynasty. They are on exhibition in the Chopsticks Hall of Shanghai Folk Arts Museum.

The knife sheath (below) has two sides. One side is veneered with hawksbill and the

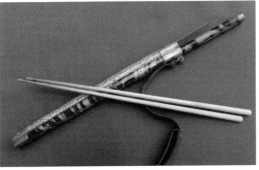

Chopsticks in knife sheath of the Qing Dynasty

other is veneered with ivory. On the ivory side, four hawksbill horses are inlaid, while on the hawksbill side four ivory horses are inlaid. Attached to the chopsticks are long metal toothpicks.

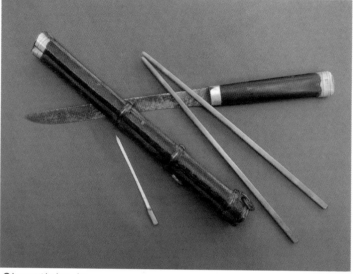

Chopsticks in sheath veneered with sharkskin

This (above) is a sheath veneered with sharkskin and four copper rings around it. Its outside pocket holds a pair of 24-centimeter-long ivory chopsticks.

The two pairs of chopsticks (page 92) are 21.5 centimeters long, the top and bottom parts veneered with ivory and the middle part walrus tusk. They are called Mandarin duck chopsticks, also known as husband and wife chopsticks. They look the same at first glance but if one takes a careful look, he will find one pair has 3 centimeters of ivory veneered at one end while the other pair has only 2 centimeters.

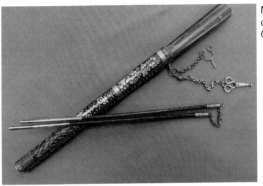

Mother-of-pearl chopsticks of the Qing Dynasty

Jiading bamboo carving has a history of four hundred years. A famous craftsman did the carving on these chopsticks and the cover (page 94, upper) was embroidered specially by the bride. On the front of one pair was carved poetic verses like "Good birds in tree branches are also friends. Flowers falling on water make a good story." Carved on the back was the picture of *Zhuge Liang Making Use of Eastly Wind to Win a Battle*. On the front of the other pair were characters announcing "The heart is like gold just as is the fragrance

Sheath chopsticks with patterns of twin fish of the Qing Dynasty

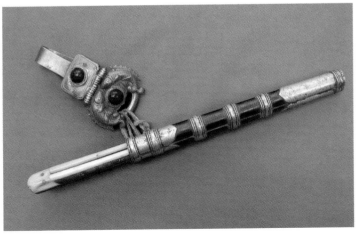

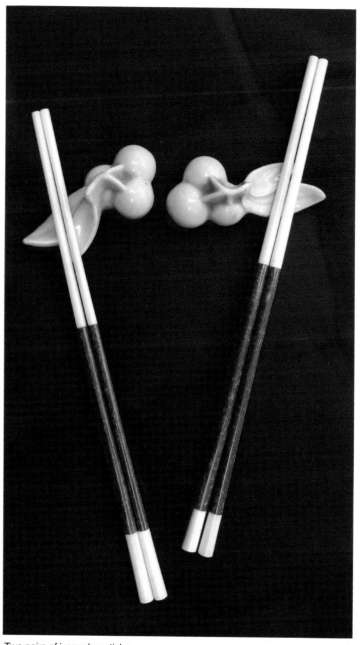

Two pairs of ivory chopsticks
of the Qing Dynasty

Xiang courtesan bamboo chopsticks veneered with silver of the Qing Dynasty

of the orchid". On the back was carved the picture of Emperor Ming of the Tang Dynasty Touring the Moon Palace.

The chopsticks are only seven centimeters long, so they are not for eating meals but an auspicious ornament to speed up labor for women giving birth in regions south of the Yangtze River. When the newly married gets pregnant, her mother would order that little chopsticks with silver chain be made to send

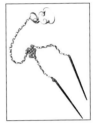

Ebony chopsticks of the Qing Dynasty

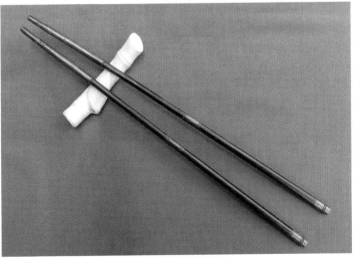

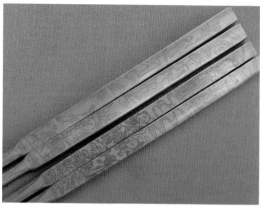

Twin pairs of bamboo chopsticks with Jiading style carving of early last century in Shanghai

to her daughter's family, in the hope that her daughter gives birth safely and soon. After the baby is born, the little chopsticks will be left with the baby as a toy as well as a good omen to prevent mishap.

Extraordinarily long hardwood chopsticks

Extraordinarily long hardwood chopsticks: these chopsticks (left) are 199.8 centimeters long. They were exclusively made in memory of the tenth anniversary of the Chopsticks Hall of Shanghai Folk Arts Museum in 1998. The pair weighs 7.5 kilograms and sets a record of the longest chopsticks in China.

This one (below) is different from ordinary

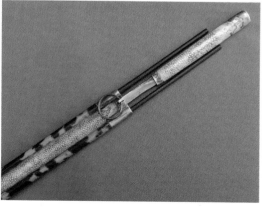

Chopsticks in hawksbill sheath of the Qing Dynasty

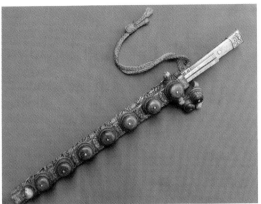

sheath chopsticks, which holds a knife in the main sheath and chopsticks in the attached. The sheath holds the knife in the middle with two small hawksbill holders on each side for chopsticks. The chopsticks, made of ebony, are 24 centimetres long.

Mostly the Mongolian and Manchu people use chopsticks in sheaths. The Tibetan chopsticks in sheath are rare, particularly with its

Eight tools for eating crabs of the Qing Dynasty

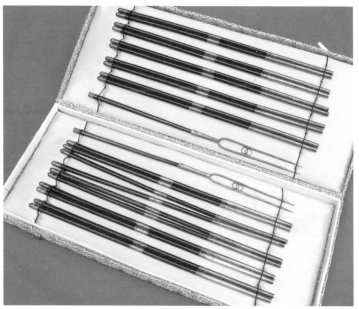

Coral chopsticks
with silver inlaid of
the Qing Dynasty

extraordinary length of 42 centimeters.

The so-called eight tools for eating crabs (previous page) are recorded as being created in the Ming Dynasty, including hammer, swage, pincers, spade, spoon, fork, scraper and needle. The eight tools of my collection are roughly the same with a few different tools, including hammer, swage, pincers, spoon, axe,

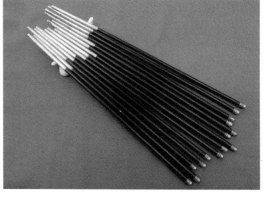

Ebony chopsticks
with silver inlay of
the Qing Dynasty

scraper, chopsticks and hook. In the Qing Dynasty, there were also four tools, six tools or ten tools for eating crabs. They were made of copper and not easily broken.

Ten-piece dining tools box of the Qing Dynasty

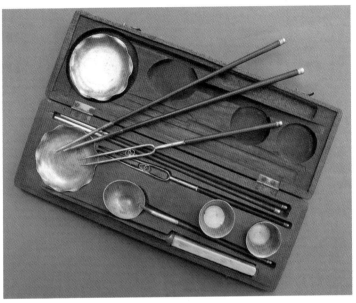

Twin pairs of red-painted chopsticks with double-happiness design of the Qing Dynasty

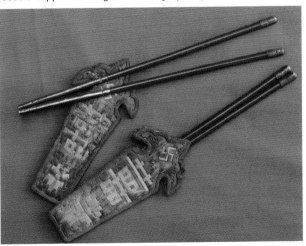

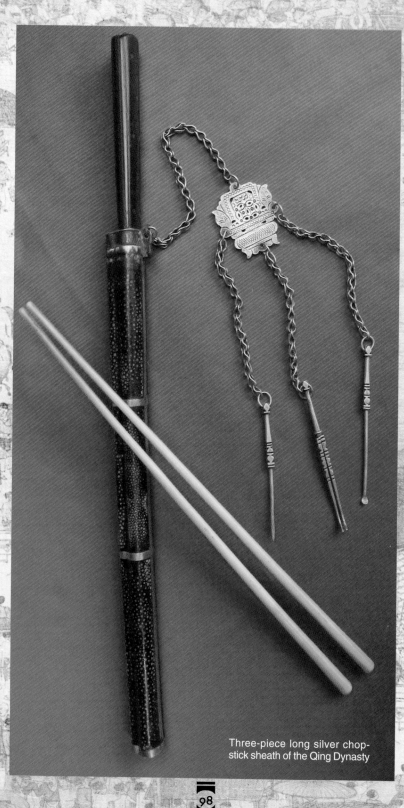

Three-piece long silver chop-stick sheath of the Qing Dynasty

Chopstick sheath with silver threads of the Qing Dynasty

Chopstick sheath with
turquoise decoration of
the Qing Dynasty

Mr. Lan Xiang inside his personal chopstick museum

图书在版编目（CIP）数据

中国筷子／蓝翔编著．－北京：外文出版社，2005.

ISBN 7－119－03852－4

Ⅰ．中⋯ Ⅱ．蓝⋯ Ⅲ．筷－文化－中国－英文 Ⅳ．TS972.23

中国版本图书馆 CIP 数据核字(2004)第 116937 号

编　　著：蓝　翔

翻　　译：陈　林

插　　图：李士伋

设　　计：元　青等

责 任 编 辑：兰佩瑾

中国筷子

© 外文出版社

外文出版社出版

（中国北京百万庄大街 24 号）

邮政编码：100037

外文出版社网页：http：//www.flp.com.cn

外文出版社电子邮件地址：info@flp.com.cn

sales@flp.com.cn

北京大容彩色印刷有限公司印刷

中国国际图书贸易总公司发行

（中国北京车公庄西路 35 号）

北京邮政信箱第 399 号　邮政编码 100044 作

2005 年 1 月(24 开)第 1 版

2005 年第 1 版第 1 次印刷

（英）

ISBN 7－119－03852－4

05200 （平）

7－E－3642P